A Tea with Shostakovich

in case of emergency press

We are proud to acknowledge the Traditional Owners of country throughout Australia and to recognise their continuing connection to land, waters, and culture.

We pay our respects to their Elders past, present, and emerging.

We support recognition, reconciliation, and reparation.

in case of emergency press

http://www.icoe.com.au

A Tea with Shostakovich

Fulvio Tramontano

Published by In Case of Emergency Press 2021

ISBN 978-0-6485571-9-7

*Dust jacket and title page photo by **engin akyurt** on Unsplash*

Table of contents

A dream?
I wake up and nothing
was is
real

No dream is ever just a dream.   .

I

(later before
As You Like It)

A misty gavotte of violets and wine

in wintry Prague.

Nikolett says something from the Magical
Bridge

but I don't hear.

Too late for love,

Niki,

I lost my way to Kanyakon,

the long canines silent sphinx

in a sultry maze of merciful tigers

and now I am watching a woman with no name

brushing her dark hair

so softly so smoothly

so close to me.

It is dusk, the quandary hour

so dear to morbid poets.

Tea time with Dmitri Shostakovich.

In this Baltic tea room

everything is red:

chairs, velvets, teapots, biscuits

and my mom is just a peasant,

you know,

nothing special,

her English is bad.

Reckless daughter,

Your mother is a Queen of dazzling beauty.

I still see

her veiled tongue

waving so softly

when she said

"Tartu".

Kooky paintings

are watching us.

Another cup of tea, Dmitri Dmitriyevich?

With pleasure, my dear Loveless.

Snow outside.

A drop of red milk?

Sure.

Red milk is served.

Shostakovich watches me like a bird

In Russia human life is nothing

was nothing

less than nothing

dust

is.

A sip of tea,

A piece of paper.

A pencil.

Write, write my music.

No, Dmitri.

You know.

You can't.

We can't.

Let's take a walk, *tovarish*.

Coarse laughs yells of dread

they shoot you at the nape of neck,

no advice, a gift for a child

concrete halls

dark&shot

gallows and whip when milk is spilt

ev'ry punishment is Will-o'-the-wisp.

I feel ridiculous

Napoleonic fireman helmet,

idiot glasses.

Crunchy castanets nose thumbings

I send postcards to myself

how quick the Soviet postman is?

the Little Father has just slipped

on his own cherry vomit

smutty warm floor

cigars and spits

the old rabid dog

grumbling *Yalushka… Vod… oh… Vod…
Negodyai!*

is deposed on a wet bed.

lives

courtesans sprinkle bad vinegar with sweaty
hands

die die die

dreadful hope

I still shiver

This is fear.

What's the point?

So proud of it.

Not a pale Etonian thrilled to be a Red I am

a Communist a picture of Leningrad siege,

twelve men over the roof.

My fireman uniform

cuirassier helmet

short-sighted face.

Fire is off

a pump in my hands

placid gardener,

watering calmly his beloved peonies.

My kid, my symphony

Net khleba dlya orkestra

they starve and play

Net khleba dlya orkestra

they starve and play

sturdy brass players wilt

and die

trumpets fall on trembling floor -

grey beasts are bombing.

Quartet. A quartet. My quartet.

skew the corners

Allegro

oh cantankerous

knotty and

Allegro

those

tricky turnarounds

Allegro

Allegro Agitato

I grab a canon

a crab canon I my

tea

is

cold

now.

Can she excuse my wrongs

with virtue's cloak?

A cute serf, ready to strangle a Greylag goose,

sings quietly an auld song.

Dost thou know John Downland, my little
cherry?

Knoweth this, Your Grace.

Hide, lambkin, hide.

She croaks and flees.

Becky the Chubby pops up,

slaughtering something with a twinkling hook.

Go to hide.

Don't you smell the reek of rotting light?

What about the daisies?

They died, Mine Own Lord, she smiles.

Too cold for them.

Do they need warm?

Everything needs Loveth, Mine Own Lord.

Can a daisy coronet survive in a dry icebox?

asparagus milk

eggs struggling the filthiest of death

pig head lemons

medical dead herbs

crumbs.

Icebox is just a cold blue coffin.

Your coronet has sunk

in a pot of murky water

slowly.

Unborn Loveths share a common fate, Mine
Own Lord.

silence

muddy darkness

a firework of regrets.

(She flees. A painting starts talking)

*Vous avez très bien éduqué vos serviteurs, M.
Loveléss.*

La paysanne a tué cette oie très gracieusement.

Marie Antoinette, Queen of Sorrow and
Politesse.

Pardonnez-moi monsieur, je ne l'ai pas fait exprès,

You said

after stepping on executioner foot,

So it was.

Just a hazy memory of that day.

People spitting

yelling yelling yelling

Guillotine a black cathedral

I watch the wicker basket

it waits.

The painting is quaint:

the Queen by Mupond,

throwing pebbles into the fetid water like a
toddler.

*Mon Ami, êtes-vous vraiment le Seigneur
Sansamour?*

En français ça sonne mieux.

Votre amour perdu arrive.

(cet endroit est nocif).

She puts a paper boat into the marsh,

blows over it and here's my grumpy gazelle.

High cheekbones, nervous thinness

a smile too large and

something of Japanese in her appearance,

just a bit,

just a little bit

why?

don't say my dear can't say

oh loveless you are so funny

for-give love-less for-get

bathed in the icy calm of horror

I gently place the handset on the receiver

forget loveless

past for-give

together we are

again

for-get

love-less

just forgive

I'm back

with you

for

ever

this is the cruellest of dreams

this is reality the sweetest

where is Shostakovich?

what a boring mates you have

fill my cup please

I'm thirsty

thirsty of bloody tea

where have you been all this time?

in your heart

I never left it.

Outside school

joking with the schoolboys

you say too loudly something silly

about the teacher

I put kidding my hand on your mouth

to silence you

to skim your lips

you kiss secretly my palm Hocus Pocus

The Queen of Harridans,

Empress of Shores,

Madame La Merde,

is on the watch in the piggery,

snarling with her rotten teeth

shoddy Carolina leaf.

midnight

a sleepless sow

rolls herself in her thickly filthy branch

toothless queen

opens the mouth and

yeeeeeeeeeels blind awake unspeakable horror

ugly childish scorpion voice

it was just a dream

you dizzy spectre

it was just a dream

you seeker of Loveth

a smelly smashed crab on a dirty beach

II

A dream?

I wake up and nothing

was is

real

no dream is ever just a dream

on a chair

a pigeon-coloured lamp

on a yellow bed

me

I get up

my gloomy chubby face on the mirror

*wAkEuPhUmAnBeInG/WaKeUpHuMaNbEiNg/w
Ak!?*

I choke the clock.

Where is my love?

(come on, boy, cut it out)

All right,

Queen of Bitches,

Bitch of Queens,

Hang me, hang me and then

Hide, hide my corpse

In a cheap wooden coffin

And bury, throw it away,

Away

in the harsh holy sandy Mina soil

Boundless Kingdom of my Early Childhood.

last wish a lash

for each couple

salivating, proudly snogging

over coffin-coloured

peeled benches

in a triumphal waste

of time

spit

and happiness

a whiplash

for each time

I killed my screen,

unable, just unable

to watch inside

the Upper Fucking Side apartment.

Well-polished furniture.

Books.

Hockney on the green wall.

Witty conversations.

Iced wine

French food

Spotless tablecloths

They eat and laugh.

Sofas, cuddles, jazz.

Kisses, bed.

Then troubles then rain then tears.

Then kisses and kisses again.

Then stop.

Then End.

Then End.

Ballymun.

A mall.

Testing bed

before they wed.

Let's marry in the shade

gosh it's posh

eleven oaks around Mudpond

a swarm of trilly damsels

awaiting the misfortune bouquet.

Nice people, isn't it?

Purple hogs and a rat

In the chapel with a cat

And a yellow flapping bat

Ego conjungo vos in matrimonium.

In nomine Patris, et Filii,

et Spiritus Sancti.

Amen.

lousy music

yelling kids

mirrors

loving kittens

persuaded to be eternal

hand in hand

shop smile eat kiss drink

Who shall be the widow?

I bet.

I win.

III

Rainy evening.

Slow Tube.

A copy of free Daily Ignoramus

on my knees:

"RATS ON THE WAY!"

A ghost vessel,

stuffed with thousands of cannibal rats,

inexorably approaches Ireland.

I stifle politely a belch.

Page four.

Amid a labyrinth

of tits and heels

I find at least a chess puzzle:

Puzzle of the day

White to play.

Wrong metric.

A fat lady quietly snores besides me.

"It was a tricky ending,

involving a couple of knights"

My solution is wrong.

Mudchute.

Listless rain.

What's the time?

The fat lady fled.

Ticket inspector is a cute Asian girl.

我想嫁給中國人

Why not?

IV

Slow Tube.

Mugginess.

an-ger

too

sleepy

for

fu-rour

now

is

ev'ry

thing

too late

to whip

ˈsʌm-wʌn

sleep

love-less

sleep

di'el'er is lulling you so sweetly

for-get

a mumbo jumbo love of dream

Kat for-get

her ghost

is lost

have a nap

fall asleep

fall asleep

V

Along the soft banks

of murky Mekong

the Beautiful Harlot

draws lazy circles

into mossy water

with her ivory foot.

No mercy,

no mercy at all.

Circles are bigger,

weaker.

She smiles.

Silence,

my darling,

no love,

just silence.

About the Author

Fulvio Tramontano is an Italian writer. He has published three books: *La casa sull'oceano (2002), L'innocenza di Gabo Stark (2009), Vietato fumare oppio negli ascensori (2014).*

www.ingramcontent.com/pod-product-compliance
Lightning Source LLC
Chambersburg PA
CBHW022001130726
47903CB00014B/2700